THE ART OF GARDENING

for my father

To Pat
with my love and thanks

THE ART OF
GARDENING

Mary Robinson

Mary Robinson

FlambardPress

First published in Great Britain in 2010 by Flambard Press
Holy Jesus Hospital, City Road, Newcastle upon Tyne NE1 2AS
www.flambardpress.co.uk

Typeset by BookType
Cover Design by Gainford Design Associates
Front cover painting: Detail from 'Midsummer Day' by Jenny Cowern,
used by kind permission of Raymond Higgs
Printed in Great Britain by Cpod, Trowbridge, Wiltshire

A CIP catalogue record for this book is available from the British Library.

ISBN: 978-1-906601-14-0

Flambard Press wishes to thank Arts Council England
for its financial support.

Flambard Press is a member of Inpress.

The paper used for this book is FSC accredited.

Contents

The museum

This solitary juggernaut of bones
for ever balanced on the marble plain
looms above me.
Light filters through the opaque roof
hen coop wire trapped in glass.
I clutch the stout cardboard ticket
comfortingly firm
date and number cleanly stamped.
The bulk of this building unnerves me
I am breathing inside a stone monster.
I listen to the sounds –
chiselled clicks of a man's steel-tipped heels
the shoosh of my rubber-soled sandals
whispers that scuttle round the silent body
like a mouse.

Everything is watching me – the walls,
the dinosaur, the attendant in the next room.

Suddenly
amid the basement's classical columns
Humperdinck's *Hansel and Gretel* roars
on a giant pianola, baroque machines
burst into life, steam engines
are fired, brass pistons plunge, everywhere
belts and flywheels flail like a fantastic
Emett animation.
The smell of metal polish, whale-oil lubricant,
the damp of my father's harris-tweed jacket
(a whiff of the Western Isles, coasters,
seaweed, mines, quarries).
In his pocket the clip of a biro
catches the light
as he bends down to usher me
into the same magic quarter
of the revolving door.

Seal

We skitter
past derelict mine workings,
scratch through gorse –
its yellow flowers
spicing the spring air –
and leap the last stone steps
to the shore.

They're ahead of me,
tearing off clothes,
printing the soft sand
with their feet
gasping and shrieking
as their winter skin
hits the nacreous sea.

They swim
with youth's easy grace.
The cove's gentle arms
enclose them.
A black float
off the headland
marks where men drown
their pots each night.

A dark head glistens –
they are joined
by another. No one
sees or hears him arrive.
They tread water and watch
a whiskered face
shining fur
heavy shoulders
the plectrum eyes of an old man.

Weeks later, walking
past uncut oats and kale,
I hear seals out on the skerries
half a mile away.
Ghostly, amelodic,
their voices
not a lament or cry
but a cantata

of abstract sound.
The music
of sea caves and tide race,
singing for the days
we hide inland.
I think of storms
and my two sons asleep
sailing on a sea of dreams.

Distant music

She is a time traveller, marooned
in a twenty-first century of CDs and holiday snaps.
By chance she has survived –
collodion chemicals sending her image
on a trajectory into tomorrow.

A slim wooden box, covers still smelling of leather,
tiny bill-hook clips freckled with verdigris –
it could be a small notebook. Inside
there is just one page of her life
written with light.

She is placed for a portrait, posed for posterity
one arm resting on a spiral-legged table
her fingers hanging like quavers beamed with bone.
She wears her best dress, velvet trim,
feathered with lace at wrist and neck.

WFB's mother – Caroline A. Ball
Died March 14. 1869.

Her chromosomes leave a trace
in the shape of a mouth, a soft slumped jaw,
those large deep-set eyes of her great-great-grandsons
but mostly she has imprinted on her descendants
that gaze –

serious, resigned, looking up and away
hearing distant music.
She is like a bird – a lark perhaps,
singing her skein of genes
into the future.

Recollecting water

White noise pours from the earth –
a liquid meteor shower.
Meadowsweet almonds the air.
I crush watercress with gritty sandalled feet,
brambles snag my ankles and I know
there will be a scabbed tear of scar next day.

I splay my hand as a sieve – splashes
darken the threads of my cotton shirt,
smear beige streaks on earth-brown legs.
I'm doused with the spring's strength
as its rainbow arc spurts to the stream
plashy with mint and rushes.

The flow forces the jug down,
water spills up and over before I can stop,
droplets poise on the rim.
I carry it back to the house,
curl one hand round the haft's sharpness
and finger the scallop shapes engraved on the glass.

A pool of stillness lies at the table's centre
as clear as the Waterford chandelier
above the staircase in the sisters' house.
A miniature spring pours from the jug's lip –
I taste sunlight so cold it stings my teeth
and scalds my throat.

I've kept the jug.

Mirror

Dawn and sunset and the light between
hair unravelling out of sleep,
toothpaste, Listerine and lipstick,

dust from memory's wings,
a little stain like lichen –
amalgam's claws scratching,

and my mother,
shrouding it with a shawl
lest lightning should strike.

Girl with a lamp

I watch the flare of a new mantle,
incandescent gauze, more fragile
than a moth's wings;
I spell a lexicon of light's incantations –
Aladdin, paraffin, Tilley, hurricane,
wick, alive with a fragment
of Promethean fire; I inhabit
a lampscape of flame and shade.

I will be away when the electricity comes, wires
strung like washing lines
across the fields. At the back of the cupboard
the lamps will huddle together
like workmen dismissed.
But my mother's wish will be granted.

Tape measure

In memory of my maternal grandfather

A half moon headstone
and a green bolster.
No photograph
but I see you
in your workroom
the tape looped
round your shoulders
when everything
was made
to measure.

You lived
on the ragged edge
of the village – tailors
always soft or worse –
with cats
and a stray cur.

You died too soon.
I cannot measure
the distance
between us
but I hear you say
Off the peg
from places
I only knew
on the school-room globe.

My mother
had your tape
but not your gift
for making.

Parachute silk
never metamorphosed
into slips
and nightgowns,
the sewing machine
stayed locked
in its wooden ark,
the key
strung on the handle.

After her death
I found
among her sewing things
shoved in an old biscuit tin
with spools of thread
tangled like fishing nets
wrecked by a storm,
that fading ribbon
of yards and inches
each end tipped
with a metal tag
like a thumbnail's
half moon.

Apple blossom

Don't go my mother said
standing under the apple blossom
wearing that long baggy cardigan
snagged and pilled like a neglected paddock.

How could we not go?
I was doing a last round of the house
checking for something forgotten
but in reality saying farewell.

The removal men had gone.
I looked out of the wash-house window
and there she was, unchanged
after twenty years.

The spring before I started school
she had shown me the alphabet
under the apple tree – pale petals fell on the paper
as she traced the shapes with her self-taught hand.

Years later I was reading my own books.
In the evenings she banged out campaigning letters,
the old manual typewriter resounding to the clack
of rage and the rasping roller of frustration.

Now my last sight of her will always be
under the apple tree –
Don't go she said.

If it's spring –

I should be in the grey house on the hill
with blue slates rippling across the roof
a wave of pebbledash against the wall
blackthorn which nobody planted in flower
a curlew's fluting cadence in the fields
and light glancing off scrap cars at Gilfach –

knowing I had eternity to write
and all my life ahead.

Reunion

That weekend all rails and roads led there. The train stopped between
    stations –
'points and signalling failure' – a litany of mobile phones

and fractious children; scattered ox-eye daisies in the ballast
like a Mary Quant print. Unsettling clouds moved across the window.

Changing at Preston video screens disintegrated
into electronic rain. In the car we were awkward,

snatched safe phrases. We arrived and saw the garden at dusk:
the suburb's woodland shades – herb bennet, red campion ('60s pink),

enchanter's nightshade, a bee feeling its way along a stem freighted
with rain drops (that dubious balance between gravity

and surface tension). After the meal, softened by wine, we talked
long into the dark – a strange odd-numbered game of verbal tennis.

We looked into that cavern of crumbling rocks which is the past,
when Armstrong and Aldrin rambled on the moon, America

was fighting in Vietnam – and now the whiplash of time brings round
another war. In the cathedral we once heard Menuhin play Bach,

cheap choir-stall seats so close we sensed the music fluttering
in his veins. Like women everywhere our talk is mainly

family and friends. Five of us, seventeen children. Exams,
weddings, aged parents, work. One delves into her heart, 'I gave up

everything for my children.' The rest of us resist the years'
intent to shunt us to the margins. The following day we wake

to a jaded garden, devoid of street-lamp glamour. Buildings refuse
to recognise us, treat us like ghosts. A whole generation

of trees, like adults not seen since childhood, renounces us.
We try barred doors, remember the student sit-in (someone's

now a professor). Another garden – Sunday lunch – Victorian
shrubbery – lush and purpling with rhododendrons, an iris

I have never seen before, a black-and-white cat pouncing
on the air a butterfly has just displaced. We sprawl

on chairs and steps. I talk to a friend's daughter, recovering
from glandular fever, looking forward to the autumn.

The last day of summer

How the sea draws us
as we walk down the rough track.
You give me bilberries
with your hand cupped to my mouth.
We reach the end of the land

watch light undressing
the sea's silk, the silver clasps
of islands. We are
silent, as if love could start
on the last day of summer.

Shelling peas

The pod's seam yields with a crack

she leans back in her chair
her spine relaxing after a day's work

she eases her thumbnail along its length

strands of hair blow across her mouth
a swallow's shadow touches her body

tearing until it is hinged like a razor shell

the garden lifts its heavy coat of green and sighs
roses and spearmint

ending in a husk of dry leaves

she lifts a ringless hand to her face
and smells the crushed pods

peas fall like hail into a bowl.

Heart Wood

Wounding the heartwood
the blade cuts deep

time pulls the heart apart
smudges the letters

he plants his grief
in the shape of a heart

the leaves' laughter
spills over the wall

a memory hoard
in the heart wood.

Fall

The beech tree is aground, the leaves' stomata
brush the road, bark rusts over harpoons
of barbed wire and roots still suck soil
and stones. I can see into its heart,
its secret record of peace and war.

It reminds me

of the whale in the museum
rendered to the grandeur of its bones
suspended from the roof, filling the room,
and I leaned from the gallery and touched
the stiff fronds which once sifted the sea's krill.

This crazy time of year

when weather's tossed up, mixed and scattered,
we're all out there, looking for firsts –
lambs, violets, a peacock butterfly
faded from the flight through winter
but giving life another go.

It's a rickety spring – meltwater,
mudwater filling the hoofprints,
yet everything jostling for the start.

Trees limber up for another season –
try out a few bobbles of buds,
sallows mist over with pollen,
blackthorn lingers in monochrome flowers
near abandoned farms.
Hail scums a pond like blossom.

In sandy fields ribbed with green
lapwings tumble, polishing
their wit by constant repetition.

Narcissi and jonquils strumpet
unnatural colours in the garden.
Like the helicopter which checks the pipe line every Tuesday
a bumblebee manoeuvres round the flowering currant.
Coltsfoot clapperclaws its way through tarmac
before it fizzes with a froth of seeds
and starts again for next year.

For a moment it's all glitter and mirror
and I watch the sky, craving
a returning swallow or martin.

Hedges green over, eager to heal
the slashed split ends of winter;
gorse, with careless irony, shows gold.
And underneath are drifts of wood anemones
like sweepings from star factories in the sky.

Crane

'The crane, that has totally forsaken this country, bred familiarly in our marshes.'
    Thomas Pennant, *Zoology* (1768)

Water silts into one grazing level, fields breathe
the sweet smell of cattle inked against a sky's torn edge.

A rare vagrant hieroglyph, vertical in a flat land,
picks gobbets out of this water-meadow soup.

In every language it is guttural – *grus grus, garan, crane,*
gru, geranion. But this one has a mandala's silence:

feathers ash-grey as burnt paper, red eyes to scan me,
the dowdy bustle of a dancer with no partner.

It struggles to take off, dragging chains of myth –
constellation, satellite, heavenly messenger,

harbinger of spring; a young girl folding paper cranes –
strange pilgrimage for her feather-tipped fingers.

Dandelion

Soft fontanelle of flower
geodesic gossamer
puffball of light

one day everything is green and yellow
a week later a million poised parachutes
strain between delay and departure

a child's view of time
1   2   3   4   5   6   7   8   9   10
fragile indestructible ephemeral

these clocks belie the sundial's hours
tell the blowing child of freedom
seeds floating into the future

whirligig of hairs reaching out
each fruit hooked
to lodge in the earth

lion's tooth root devouring time

Migrant

There are places
> that call us each year –

the valley held taut
> by the mountains

with no issue
> but the sea

where the sand
> shimmers with mica

and we tread
> the old track to the village

catching
> the background rasp

of insects
> in the reeds,

a pair of geese
> backlit against the water,

and I realise
        that what we hear,

as the marsh marigolds
        fix the faltering

sun's last light
        are not insects at all,

but grasshopper
        warblers reeling,

and I wonder
        if you will ever

return.

Summer lane

meadow buttercups, their yellow crockery
spinning in the wind

parasols of pignut and cow parsley
with their umbelliferous fringe

wild roses – no one innocently bridal anymore
but if she was it would be the wild rose

clover pompons made lopsidedly by the playgroup in
(an unfortunate) pink (which no one wants) and white wool

plain plantain flowers could be stylish
were it not for railway shades of brown and cream

heath-spotted orchids – how our northern latitude
adapts the exotic

fragrance of dried grass just occasionally
the hayfields are not abandoned

the heat of a hundred summer walks
swirling around my legs

hooves sounding the road
like a ghost from the past

Swallows

All summer they painted the ceiling of the sky
with their invisible inky scribbles
their droppings spattered the wall
at night I would hear the feed me/need me
cries of the chicks and wake to them at first light.
They raised three broods under our roof
birding the air with swallows.

This morning the sky was as calm as the lake at dawn
the trees and hedges 2D stage flats in the mist
swallows were lining up on the telephone wires
nudging and chittering like prommers in a ticket queue.
After a summer of carefree cartoons
it was time for some serious drawing –
an arc linking two hemispheres.

The sky has cracked open with their absence
tonight the wind rattles the leaves
I turn on the radio and hear news of another season
of war gathering on the horizon.
But one day after the long siege of winter
I will catch sight of a ghost

from another year ribboning above the stream.
The next day there will be the print of a small
bird skating on the chill air.

Vanessa atalantis

They are like a Mozart fantasia –
each one an elegant fluttering phrase
Vanessa atalantis: red admirals

on red apples, the flesh browned to a sponge
within the torn skin. Decay sweetens the air.
One red eye glows in each smoky underside.

Sated they rest in the still air, on white towels on the line,
on plastic wrapping on a scrap boiler,
black-plated wings, red stripe, white patches, steel-blue trim.

Chill nights herd them south,
not migration but irruption, a volcanic cloud
drifting to the Mediterranean. A speck of butterfly ash

has blown into my study –
a memento mori all winter long. In spring
it will open with the apple blossom.

November

November. No frost.
Summer's seeds
are growing
out of season.

At eleven
I dig parsnips'
white bones
from the earth.

In a pavement crack
a poppy flowers.
Bible-paper petals
wisp in the wind.

Swans skid down
on the firth
where once Catalinas
moored for Atlantic patrol.

Robin

Why is it that, in the last month of the year
when I walk to the post box by the stone house
where roses still bloom over the window,

I remember a boy one winter's day
holding out his fingers like wing tips
for a robin, which – instead of keeking
behind a haw curtain – came to his hand
for crumbs and, when it flew back to the thorns,
its feathers dusted his skin as softly
as the first snowflakes?

Carol

At the year's end
a candle –
sunlight splinter,
flame petal –
the wick a dark stamen
tipped with red,

between my fingers skin
membraned with light

and I recall
the yellow flowers
of summer –
bird's foot trefoil,
St John's wort,
archangel.

Augustine sees Ambrose reading silently

My tongue was filled with questions I knew he could answer:
his door was wide and he was alone –
on the table a book and a half-eaten hunk of bread.
The light from the high window bent over him like grace.
His mouth, soft and full, did not open
and the fine hair on his upper lip was still.
I saw his finger trace each line,
the only sound a whisper of skin on vellum
where a scribe had scratched out an error.
He was reading in the Book of the Lord.

I was dumb with silence and returned to my house.
I heard children's voices playing in a garden
as I turned the first page.
I put a grape in my mouth to stop my eager tongue.
I did not notice the slave
when he came to tend the lamps
or taste the wine he brought me.
As I closed the book the sun was rising over the city.
Now I understand
reading is an act of faith – *tolle, lege.*

Aldus Manutius

Venetian master printer c.1450–1515

Here is my *Virgil.*

You look amazed that something so small
contains the whole *Aeneid.*
Alchemy? Yes, an alchemy that can take
a beggar's rags and change them into paper
as white as swans on the Lagoon.
The cover is soft calfskin – feel it –
will it not fit in the pointed sleeve of your gown?

Forget those old books kept in locked rooms,
chained like great beasts at a fair. Beautiful, of course,
but heavy as lead on the cathedral roof.
Surely you have noticed the mistakes –
a monk whose mind no doubt was elsewhere – on food, or sleep
or an illicit love. And you can smell
the mice before you find the lacuna
they have gnawed in the vellum.

You want to know about printing? Come,
I will show you.

Here is Francesco – see how he takes the tools
in his long goldsmith's fingers and cuts away
base metal to leave the letters proud.
The Doge's ring is not more beautiful.
The letters are backwards? Forgive my laughter!
They are perfect – Francesco never makes mistakes.

Look at these tiny moulds – yes, touch them with your fingertips
like a blind child. Can you imagine what happens next?
You seem concerned about the furnace – step back a little.
See the molten metal pours like honey
into the moulds.

Over here the new type swarms in a straw skep
waiting for the man we call the compositor.
No, he won't answer you, for we speak only Greek here.
Watch, as he sets letters in the frame,
the honeycomb from which Virgil's sweetness comes.

I am pleased you esteem the *typeface* –
I want the words to *run*,
each letter leaning forward to touch
its neighbour, like men hastening to the harbour,
eager for news when a ship after a long voyage
returns home.

I did not know you were a navigator.
You can read my books anywhere –
on the Rialto, on a boat, in the shade of a tree
in a new found land. I too am a discoverer –
remember my mark: the dolphin and anchor.

The Egoist

Harriet Shaw Weaver 1876–1961

Remember, Mr Ellmann, I published
Portrait – that was how it started. And I
believed in him.

At first I was 'The Monro Client'.
I sometimes wonder what would have happened
if Mr Joyce and I had never met,
if I had kept my shy grey self concealed.
I sent my nun-in-profile photograph –
I ended up as his confessor.

One holiday in Penrith, buttoned-up
and woollen-gloved, my mouse hair brushed and bunned,
I wrote him my commission: *one full-length
grave account of his esteemed Highness
Rhaggrick O'Hoggnor's Hogg tomb as per
photos enclosed.*

        And any day I could hear
wicked gossip, and Mr Monro moaned
about the money and the drinking (he
forgot the once-paupered cannot but spend).

I would catch the boat-train, watch the lightning
tear the dark horizon on stormy crossings.
Paris. Hotels. His birthday when I sat
becardiganed upon the sofa while
the party carousel spun round me.

The last visit almost snapped the thread that bound us.
Of course I minded! But I never wavered.
He was knocked up by life and carping critics.

Oh, that commission, Mr Ellmann? Yes –
to find it, open his last book and read.

What did I receive? The work in progress,
explanations, *Ulysses* (copy No. 1),
manuscripts, confidences, letters – so
many letters. It was quite simple –
I gave him money, he gave me his wordswork.

Shakespeare and Company

Sylvia Beach 1887–1962

I thought I had lost my faith for always
until I met him. In the photographs they took
the shop frames us: my hair is a halo
of frizz; he with his pilgrim's ash plant looms –
even the heels of my sensible shoes
can't make me taller.
                                          Before dawn breathlessly
I met the Dijon train. It was his birthday,
an epiphany to eclipse all others.
We unveiled Darantière's parcel. Then
the title's white archipelago rose
from the cover's blue sea, *Ulysses.*
                                                              'Put not
your trust in Crooked Jesus,' Adrienne
and I would say. But when the soldier came
for the last book I refused to recant.

The Art of Gardening

Karel Čapek 1890–1938

Gardening for you was science fiction,
a surreal future where nothing added up:

you were late that year – Saint Wenceslas' Day –
and joked about a dearth of pots, a superfluity
of bulbs, disappearing compost, bone meal
not yet in stock – you kept on planting
like some crazed gardener's apprentice.

Then you locked the gate to your heart's ground.
Seeds of snow sifted against stones, the Vltava ran
gun-metal grey, soot disgraced Prague's walls.
On St Stephen's Day miners
brought flowers to your funeral.

In that long weekend before the storm
did you foresee the blighted spring, the summer
long delayed? Your tools were snapped for kindling,
a sharp knife filched, and in the street your pots
were smashed like glass.

The clock of the seasons slurs. But each time the earth
hesitates at the year's crossroads
those knuckled bulbs with papery skin split,
sprout, shoot petalled flame and open the gate
for Proserpina's flowers.

Lübeck

Instantly I recognise the Holsten Gate
from the photograph: here it is in the brick
with its double-coned hat, built for an invasion
which never happened, sinking harmlessly
into the Baltic marsh like a salt merchant's overloaded wagon.

When attack came it pitched from the sky.
In the twin-spired Marienkirche the bells
lie where they fell, fractured, tearing the brick
flesh of the floor, spilling the sound hoard of centuries.

Two hundred and thirty-six miles to Arnstadt,
less to the Polish border. Lübeck's osmosis
draws the displaced, as the plates of time and place
grind over each other.

In the street trodden by Bach
a violinist busks, plays Paganini's caprice,
highest notes a hair's breadth
within hearing.

Compelled to listen to this youth in a wraith's body,
seeing the curve of cheek bones beneath the cobweb skin,
the shadowed sockets, the crumbled
concrete dust on his clothes,
we stand, as the colours of music flame
and my heart's bell hung in its ribbed cage
falls burning.

Black bread

On the shelf at Aldi rye bread *schwartzbrot*
bread that will keep in wooden chests for weeks
bread you can eat at dawn and do a day's labour.

The sour-sweet taste of it – a snatched lunch when
we biked through July cornfields to the coast
on old Third Reich tracks, concrete white in the heat.

An ear of corn split with my thumbnail, flour
soft on my tongue. Wind turbines flailed the air.
The A of a granary's great brick gable,

tented with rye-brown thatch, swept the ground.
A peg-mill, redeemed from fire, the whole mill-house
dancing to catch the eye of the wind.

                                        And
the tracks ran on, resolute, determined,
as if the crew-cut stubble had no choice.
At Schönberg the Baltic hazed the horizon,

little whispy waves nibbled white sand
drifting against breakwaters (*nicht betreten*).
The drift of things: rye grains carried in carts,

in desperate sacks, in pockets, across
the settlers' ocean to turf roofed dugouts
to rise as prairie sourdough.

Martin Luther and the swan

In the Mariakirchen, Bergen

No guide – just a silent cleaner
working hard at God's house-keeping,
her rubber gloves flesh-coloured pink
as she dusts the glitzy altar.

Those Hanseatic merchants were
shameless: all around the pulpit
cavorts a cornucopia
of bare-breasted Bergen hussies.

You were an embarrassment, faith's
token portrait in the shadows –
black robed, the white bird at your side.

The swan was your feathered familiar –
he would take the bread from your hand
but his wing beats could stop your heart.

Grieg at Troldhaugen

How can I paint with music?
Music that has lain
locked in fjord darkness
for centuries?

Wood smoke at dusk,
earth's breath after rain,
the way water and light
resonate through glass

my longing for this place

the sugar smell
of sawn wood in every room,
album leaf,
a child's lost red mitten

the beat of my own heart

waking to the hush
of snow,
the nordlys flaring
the winter night

sweet brown goats' cheese,
fish scales' mica glitter,
a green cadence whispering
along each dal in spring

myself, wheezing like an old troll

apple blossom, children playing
under rhubarb-leaf umbrellas,
orchids and asphodel
in summer pastures

the brave frog who watches over me

a labourer whistling,
wedding dance,
springar, halling and slåtter,
drone and drum

white gulls tumbling
like snowflakes over water,
blackbird notes
on frost

and beyond the lake, the other side of silence

George Orwell on Jura

For Jane Morgan

It was a bright cold day in April

The world in tatters but everything I had planted
quick with spring – wild cherry blossom,

tight buds of tulips and narcissi,
even the tips of Eileen's rose unfurling.

I am carrying a story, lying in the bowl of my skull,
and I must take care not to spill one drop.

Under the tilted ceiling the smell of paraffin and cigarettes
and the tap of the typewriter keys like hail on glass.

I must wrest the harvest while I can, husband my energy,
shelter the crop from a nuclear winter.

When I come here I know I can live for ever.
Good health is decoration, fancy wallpaper – I can get by without it.

In old Norse this is Deer Island
and I come upon them drinking,

their feet clack the burn's stones as they move on;
or Diùra in Gaelic, something hard and enduring.

Iridescence glitters on puddles. A rickety engine,
often breaking down. I sit by the side of the road

hoping someone will come along, confident
I will get there. I slash at rushes choking the track.

False hopeful starts, ages tinkering, then suddenly it goes,
everything running smoothly – one cog or part was needed –

and I'm away, I can't stop.
There is only one direction to go – down to the shore.

The sea roads of my life lead here –
white sand and clear water with seals swimming about in it.

A spring tide and a westerly,
the outboard snatched away but somehow

spitting out brine we get to a rock
and force the old Cailleach to change her mind.

My book will be a light set on the reef of history.

Shore lines

soft as sea mist
clouds sift the light
foot marks slip into silt
salt on the tip of my tongue

waves slap and shift the shore
store of wrack and bone
one skidding stone to skim
and to atone

seabirds rend the gauze of silence
lend their cries
to a darkening land

words scratched in sand

A Journey to the Western Islands of Scotland

The journey would have seemed endless for him – that great loop round the hunchback of Scotland, seeing the Buller of Buchan, the waste of Anoch, venturing out to Skye and Coll, then waiting for days to hitch a lift on a kelp boat to Mull.

As for me, just when I've had enough of the A roads' single-track-with-passing-places, there is the pier – the ro-ro loading cars with the intricacy of a highland reel. The Calmac ferry gets under way, engines crawthumping across the Sound.

Ragwort and rhododendrons, plants he never saw, Tobermory leaching suburbia up the hillside, the Co-Op and Spar and Brown's so revered its founder has a monument looking across to the wilderness of Ardnamurchan. All else is tat and tack, something for tourists on a wet day when thrift is on vacation.

At Speinn Mor roofboxed cars crawl up the hill like mechanical snails. A low-flying jet trails war's memento mori. Orchids, heath, bog asphodel, cotton grass waving its handkerchiefs of surrender. Bootprints and metal posts rust. Black butterflies spread mourning wings. In the hollows a quietness where the moor sleeps and I must step softly or it will stir.

The country is very rough . . . we travelled many hours through a tract bleak and barren.

It's still bleak and barren, whole villages cleared. Old women remember old men who were children and saw it happen. Not history but weeping. Crofts abandoned, swathes of land ranched for sheep. Shame's fingerprints on black-house stones. Stalking – tourism's hard muscle – men in camouflage, four-wheel drives carting the kill.

But coming over the pass and seeing Loch Tuath, and Ulva spread out her skirts – the shore a lace petticoat, how could he be silent?

We were now long enough acquainted with hills and heath to have lost the emotion that they once raised . . . the first thought is to cover them with trees.

And they have. Cities of terraced firs – spaced with black ginnels – stain the hillside, now matured and ready to pulp.

Glengorm designed by a maker of chess men – an architectural version of Tenniel's *Alice* – all stepped gables, turrets, balustrades, stone globes balanced above unsuspecting heads. A tortoiseshell cat patrols the walled garden. The smell of burning rhododendrons – they are clearing them round the edge of the lawn. Japanese knotweed lurks in clumps. Imagine Victorian plant hunters . . .

As I walk to the shore Coll comes and goes in the mist. The sea deals in torn rags.
At Croig a faith of sheilings snatches summer from salt air. Here on this no-man's shore,
disputed at each tide, a detritus of fish crates *Foyle Fishery Co-Operative*
No unauthorised use, plastic bottles, nylon rope in dayglo colours no brine can fade.

On the last day I stroll to the lighthouse. The viewfinder shows Bloody Bay where
the sea ran with blood as crimson as the pool of fuschia petals on the path.
The hourly news brings Qana near. Sunlight engraves the headland.

But suddenly, just for once, the radio sows magic –
the memory is just behind the eyes, like a seahorse sleeping on its side.

Captain Cook's dinner service

Each evening, as the sky bloomed with stars,
dinner was served.
Red roses on white china
plates rimmed with gold, the edges crimped
into }s bringing together
Resolution and *Discovery*,
skirting the continent's shore,
the fractured ice by day,
by night the aurora's emerald and ruby.

It was not meant to end like this –
two ships putting into Stromness
with their cargo of grief and loss.
I could smell peat smoke
as we entered the harbour,
fish curing and late haymaking.
Linen was drying on sandstone walls
and high up a skein of geese
sailed across the sky.

Jetsam or salvage? I gave them away –
those bowls, ice cracked, dirt glued.
They kept too many memories –
blood and bone gilded with sand,
our captain's grave on a Hawaiian shore.
Now, where the slope of the hill hides
the ocean, they sleep,
safe in a glass case in the House of Skaill.

Skara Brae

a starling vanishes

into a crack

between stones

and tends her home

North Ronaldsay, Orkney

The island is a great floating meadow
a meadow with sheens of lapwings and flickering skylarks

daisies spilling pearls on grass
and in the grass curlews with scythes for beaks

marsh marigolds and dandelions coining the fields with gold
and gold-dust lichen on the Old Kirk roof

the wind puts its mouth to the stone dyke and cries
and crying an oystercatcher lifts in alarm.

They needed a shelter from that great weight of sky
a sky so heavy they paved the roofs to keep it out

slack water and a good moon and they'd be away
away over to Sanday for a dance

'Don't come back too soon' knowing the racing tide
the race that could dance them away for ever

so many lost in the war, the island merely a memory
yet the memorial clutches only one name to its heart

others left lightly, work unfinished, 'just slipping out for a
    minute'
and minutes became hours and years and exile

leaving things that might come in useful in sheds
sheddings of old stuff – batteries, wheels, an engine's bones.

The Atlantic unpicks its seams, fraying foam against rocks
sandstone rocks slabbed up like bales of cloth

black rocks on white sand are seals
seals moaning as women moan for the dead

a spirit opens the door to the wind
and the wind draws the curtain for the last time.

Fair Isle

On days like this
everything is given – .
the mail boat

slips into harbour,
grass dries as easily as linen,
angelica unfolds

its chlorophyll sheath,
windmills spin from the air
Aeolian power.

Surely winter here
is some impossible
aberration like war –

Ward Hill a film set;
the gunner's body
slumped in the ruins,

a distant figure
jerking through snowdrifts,
the lifelike screams

of women and a child.
The lighthouse beams
caress the house,

every stone and slate
alert, responding.
It was the last manned light.

Shades of Fair Isle

balewrap eggshell blue

gold-dust lichen

wren brown, ox black

ragged robin, montbretia orange

that old van no tax no MOT but still official yellow

Sterna paradisaea

He stands on the deck of the car ferry
willing the house into sight.
The croft fields are scabbed over:

memories are his mind's photographs
charting love's progress – hay, peat, fleece,
lanolin a balm to his blistered skin.

Soil has creased into his body,
his sweat, blood and semen have seeped
into the land's cracks. Here he has fathered two sons.

*

Tumbled by the world's winds
the sea swallows return.
Released into a hemisphere of light

they find the shingle tombolo, the stem
which holds the wine-glass island
brimming with sound.

A tern hovers, tail fanning, skims to its prey,
flies up – shrill coral beak, wings
a silvered vane against the sky.

Birds coeval with his sons
hatch stones with abuse
and fulfil their impossible dream.

*

Now only a string of washing flutters
the house smells of peat smoke and Black Label
his eyes water through a rainbow of absence

his emotions are raw, plucked like rooed wool –
he struggles back to the pack ice
for another winter

stern paradise.

Storm petrels at Mousa broch

A ship in the eye of the storm
petrels following, their webbed feet
pattering the waves' surface
like Peter walking on water.

Four centuries before Christ
men who built by knack and instinct
signed off their lives with a flourish –
a prescient cooling-tower shape
darkling the island sky.

Lured by earth's breath
they return and quicken
this husk of stone, birds so frail
they shuffle on crippled legs
so timid they come only at dusk.

Thousands of fluttering wings
halo this marine dovecote – its stones
churr and purr with petrels,
its inner space is musty with nests.
I could fit one on my open hand – its feathers
shades of soot but never smudging
petals of white on wing and back.

In its eyes a vortex, black
as the moon's absence.

The Poetics of Space

After Gaston Bachelard

'I am the space where I am' (Noel Arnaud)

1 The house

Architecture of the imagination
pebbles of poetry
word shelter
a box for dreaming

the body is a carapace for the spirit
as the house envelops the soul
desire pulls the mind
into word rooms

time compressed like marble
layers of settlement
shadows of dwellings
ghosted under grass

refuge amputated from the refugee
whose maimed flesh
will never forget.

2 House and universe

On a time-lapse photograph of the world at night

The beads of light are threaded round the world
like fairy lights in tawdry bars.
I scan the picture for blanks –
blue is mountains deserts forests
black is inland lakes,
the sea marbles the page with gritty school ink.

I flick a switch and imagine a world turning,
points of light joining up
like a child's dot-to-dot drawing.
My house is there somewhere
blurred in with the rest –
camp-fires street-lamps houses factories fireworks
explosions arson bombings.

Lapsed-time lithograph –
some lights are already extinguished
new ones are alight.
This photograph is a lie:
it is night all over the world
the earth snared in apocalyptic darkness
nothing will grow in this artificial glow.

All day my house has turned towards the sun
the pores of its stones soaking in heat
the skin of its paint bleaching and bubbling.
I make a last tour of the garden at dusk,
nebulae of elderflowers and wild rose in the hedge
the safe childhood smell of honeysuckle
fledged house martins swooping in ever-widening orbits
from their mud splodge under the eaves.
Above the horizon a satellite
catches the light of the setting sun
and throws it back to me.

The man who made this
has been dead for centuries –
I don't even know his name.
When I touch the wood he shaped
time is cleft apart
our hands touch across the generations.
His fingers were intimate with oak
the close-grained secrecy of wood,
divining the form latent in the forest tree –
a sapling when Gaveston was beheaded
and his lover king deposed.

The man's whole body went into this making:
the steaming breath and sweat of winter days
as the tree was lopped and barked
and finally felled.
Sawdust specks floated in cascades of light.
After the shock of dismemberment
the cord wood lay two summers,
then the rhythm of together and apart
constriction and release
every sawing followed by a seasoned resting
letting the muscles of oak relax.

This man was an alchemist –
as his chisel and knife
shaped flowers and leaves
petals of wood slipped from the grain.
He cut lines freehand
and like an unruled pencil mark
nothing is straight
but the fit never falters.
He saw a chest which glowed umber
coruscations of carving
a miracle of burning wood not consumed –
he had transformed base timber into gold.

There is a dialectic to cabinet making –
outside the beeswax surface of satin sweetness
inside the paler wood, natural, undressed
a new dimension of intimacy
secret enclosure
memory shelter
like a house within a house.
The dovetailed drawers he made
join him to me
as I open the chest
and begin to write.

4 Nests

The dream loom was broken –
'We found some torn Birds nests'
she wrote in her journal
the year of her brother's marriage;
one evening he placed the ring
on her finger to wear all night.

The nest is shaped to the bird
as the house to its lovers,
disparate clutter
woven into one piece,
swallows under the rafters
the ultimate symbiosis of nest to house.

I come back to the summer house – it breathes
deeply as I throw open the windows,
children run to the cupboard at the top of the stairs
find toys,
my hands touch once gathered wood clay straw fabric feathers
and stay for a while the unravelling dream.

Such a soft round word
for something at the cutting edge of life
a place
for breeding rearing and parting
where desire irresistible as a magnet
can turn to hate's acid etching out the heart.

5 Shells

What happens to a house when someone dies?
Imagine a line of shanty-town shacks, old camper vans,
mansions, Manhattan apartments, rustic cottages,
all gently deposited at high-water mark –
the land's offering to the sea.

I walk the sand strewn with a shamble of shells,
shelters that have outlived the sheltered,
calcareous tendrils spiralling round
shards still shirred and puckered for a perfect fit
of creature to home, inspirited stone.

Cowrie shells in the eyes of the dead,
Pope withdrawing his crazy carcass
into its grotto by the tidal Thames,
Venus on the point of stepping delicately
from her scallop boat to the shore.

Limestone vaulting into life
from waves of barley and ripples of sheepwalks
a hundred miles from salt water.
In my pocket seeds of resurrection
for my frail cockle-shell of heart.

6 Corners

There are corners of the mind

where thoughts spindrift into a parabola of dust.
Each day I move table, chairs, cutlery,
open a cupboard, hang up washing.

Behind the sheep shears and the cracked vase
sand silts against the wall –
thoughts sleep safely here, curled up in a corner.

The sun lights up a little store
of ash, fluff, seeds –
in vain keeping the heart at bay.

I find a toy's wheel, a coin,
I mend porcelain, sharpen blades
and in the garden dry seeds sprout.

7 Miniature

Everyone remembers Lilliput
(but not Brobdingnag)
the child's-eye
view which delights
taking us back
to a half-
remembered world of
the train set,
doll's house and
model village, evoking
in every grown
Gulliver moments of
tenderness, a withholding
of terrible power,
replicated in the
bird's-eye view
from the air
fading to the
horizon.

Hessian green forest –
a jay screams away
coarse bramble threads snare my feet
my mind is tangled in branches.
I walk into the past
mould grows in my lungs,
the hunted spirits slip
beneath the bark of trees.
I count my life
in rings of the cut stump.
How can I find the way
if the forest is felled?

Brown linen garden
retted with rain,
bleached by sunlight,
a robin at arm's length,
damp gritty soil in my nails
as I lift the potato's skin,
sweet sharp raspberry flesh on the tongue,
atavistic smell of cut grass.
Flanked by a paling fence
the garden must be enclosed.

Blue silk sea
light so clear it shows
every crease in the shore,
water slapping on wood, the boat wanting
the emigrant sea.
A gannet's masked face checks me
folds flatpack and hits the water like steel.
The land slackens and falls away.
My body sinks into the salt waves' heartbeat
I am sailing into the future.

9 The dialectics of outside and inside

Behind the world's back
the window's eye opens onto the land.
Light is not squandered in old houses –
first light, last light
life's borders of wood and stone.
In the slate roof a skylight
for the stars to watch
the sleepers on the bed.
When the balance of light shifts
the lamp is lit and the house waits
for the lonely traveller.

the way light rubs a curve
slip glaze brightness becoming surface matt of shadow
and always that luminous cantle at the edge of darkness

the foetal comfort of the domestic –
curtain-ring cotton-reel button basin bottle jar
objects rounding into the future

a charmed space, a private place
nailed bolted pegged
coins hidden at door-frame and window

a cabin porthole's annulet of sea
whirlpool of lighthouse stone
rare round pebble on the shore

full moon's roundel
gyroscope of gravity steadying the world's axis
cartographer's riddle

areola, iris, Leonardo's proportions of man
deranged line of eternity
a circle of angels dancing

Notes and Sources

Crane
In Japan there is a belief that if you fold a thousand origami cranes your wish will be granted. In Hiroshima Peace Park there is a statue of a young girl, Sadako Saraki, holding a folded crane. She tried to fold a thousand cranes so that her wish to return to health would be granted. She died of leukaemia at the age of twelve and her school friends completed the task.

The Egoist
Harriet Shaw Weaver published James Joyce's *Portrait of the Artist as a Young Man*, firstly in serial form in *The Egoist*, a literary review which she edited, and then in book form. Shy, intelligent, generous and frugal, in 1917 she began an anonymous benefaction to Joyce through her solicitors (Munro, Saw and Co). Joyce discovered her identity by 1920 and in 1922 they met for the first time. She gave Joyce thousands of pounds over his lifetime, paid for his funeral and was his literary executor. Richard Ellmann was James Joyce's biographer.

The lines quoted in the poem are from a letter from Harriet Weaver to Joyce (Richard Ellmann, *James Joyce*, chapter 33 (p. 582), Oxford University Press 1983 edition).

Shakespeare and Company
Sylvia Beach was the first publisher of James Joyce's *Ulysses* (printed by Maurice Darantière in Dijon). She was an American, the daughter of a Presbyterian minister, and established the Shakespeare and Company bookshop in Paris, with the help of her close friend, Adrienne Monier. Privately she called Joyce by names he had given himself, 'Crooked Jesus' and 'Melancholy Jesus'. She was interned briefly during the Second World War after refusing to sell her last copy of *Finnegans Wake* to a Nazi soldier.

The Art of Gardening
Karel Čapek was an eminent Czech writer in the 1920s and 1930s. His play *R UR* (Rossum's Universal Robots) was

successfully performed in London in 1923 and gave the English language the word 'robot'. He was a keen gardener and his book *The Gardener's Year* was reissued in English in 2004 (translated by Geoffrey Newsome, Claridge Press). He 'died of a broken heart when Czechoslovakia was handed to Germany in 1938' (*The Times* 10 April 2004).

Martin Luther and the swan
Martin Luther is traditionally depicted with a swan in Lutheran churches. The Bohemian reformer, John Huss, who was burnt at the stake in 1415, is reputed to have prophesied Luther's coming by saying 'You are roasting a goose [*hus* is Czech for goose] but after me will come a swan'.

George Orwell on Jura
George Orwell lived at the remote farm of Barnhill on the Hebridean island of Jura in the last years of his life. Here he wrote *Nineteen Eighty-Four*. He almost drowned in the whirlpool of Corrievreckan. There is a legend that the whirlpool is controlled by an old witch or *cailleach*.

The line quoted in the middle of the poem is from Orwell's description of Jura (Gordon Bowker, *George Orwell*, p. 354, Little, Brown 2003).

A Journey to the Western Islands of Scotland
Dr Samuel Johnson visited Scotland and the Hebrides in 1773 and quotations from his account are included in the poem.

Qana – a village bombed on 30 July 2006 in the Israel–Lebanon conflict. Over 60 people were killed and more than half of the casualties were children.

Captain Cook's dinner service
After Captain Cook's death in Hawaii, *Resolution* and *Discovery* made their first British landfall at Stromness, Orkney in 1780, under the command of John Gore.

Sterna paradisaea
Scientific name for the Arctic tern.

The Poetics of Space
Each poem in this sequence takes as its starting point a
chapter in *The Poetics of Space* by Gaston Bachelard
(translated by Maria Jolas, 1994 edition, Beacon Press).
The French philosopher's classic book examines how we
experience intimate places and their importance for the
imagination.

Nests
The first verse refers to entries in 1802 in Dorothy
Wordsworth's *Grasmere Journal*.

Acknowledgements

Thanks are due to the editors of the following publications in which some of these poems, or earlier versions of them, first appeared: *The Coffee House, Cumbria Life, The Eildon Tree, Envoi, Flora Facts and Fables, The Interpreter's House, Mint Sauce* (Cinnamon Press), *Moonstone, The New Shetlander, Other Poetry, Perhaps* (Cinnamon Press), *Piqué* (Templar Poetry), *Solitaire* (Templar Poetry), *The Visitors* (Cinnamon Press).

Thanks also to Cumbrian Poets for constructive criticism and encouragement.